Why be bossy?

By Janine Amos and Annabel Spenceley
Consultant Rachael Underwood

CHERRYTREE BOOKS

A Cherrytree Book

Designed and produced by A S Publishing
Design and typesetting by James Leaman and Michael Leaman

First published 2000
by Cherrytree Press, a division of Evans
Brothers Limited
2A Portman Mansions
Chiltern St
London WIU 6NR
Reprinted 2003

British Library Cataloguing in Publication Data
Amos, Janine
Why be bossy?. – (Problem solvers)
1. Social interaction – Juvenile literature
I. Title II. Spenceley, Annabel
302.1'4

ISBN 1 842 34023 9

Printed in Italy by G. Canale & C. S.p.A. - Turin

Why be bossy?

Sometimes you and your friends may want different things. Sometimes one person wants to tell everyone else what to do. That could be a problem – but you can learn to work it out together. Here are some steps to help you.

 First of all, let everyone say how they feel

 Say what the problem is

 Talk about different ways to solve the problem

 Then choose a way that makes everyone happy

The children in this book all help each other to solve problems. As you read, see if you can follow the problem-solving steps they use.

Liam and the Trees

Liam, Michel, Alice and Holly are playing Explorers.
They are deep in the rainforest.

"Let's go that way!" says Liam. "Pretend I lead you
through the jungle, where no one has ever been before!"

Michel, Alice and Holly follow Liam.

"Now we see a huge river!" Liam tells them. "We're going across."

"How?" asks Alice.

"We build a raft!" Liam answers. "Pretend we've all got axes. Start chopping down some trees, everyone!"

"We can't chop down trees!" says Alice. "There'll be nowhere for the animals to live."

"She's right!" says Holly.

"We have to – just a few, to make a raft – we must
get across!" says Liam.
"No," says Alice firmly.

"I'm the leader. That's what we do next. We have to go across!" shouts Liam.

He is feeling upset.

"You can't make us," Alice shouts back. "It's our game too!"

Alice looks at Liam.
Liam is bright red. He feels as if he will burst.
"I'm not playing!" he shouts.

Liam turns his back on his friends.
He is angry and his eyes fill with tears.

Holly goes to Mrs Casey for help.

"Liam's crying," she tells the teacher. Mrs Casey follows Holly across to the others.

"Can you tell me what the problem is?" asks Mrs Casey.

"In the game, Liam wants us to cut down trees,"
explains Holly.

"We won't. It's wrong to cut them down!" says Alice.

"We need to make a raft to get across the big river!" sobs Liam.
"I'm the leader of the Explorers. I know!"

"Yes," says Mrs Casey gently. "And your team needs to be happy with the plan, too. Can anyone think of another way to cross the river?"

"We could swim!" says Holly.
"That's too dangerous. There are crocodiles!" warns Liam.

"We could swing across on creepers!" suggests Alice.
Liam likes this idea. He starts to smile.

"Is everyone happy with that plan?" asks Mrs Casey.
"Yes!" call Liam, Michel, Alice and Holly.

Battle of the Dinosaurs

The children are making books. They are working in pairs.
  "One of you be the author and write the words," says Mrs Casey. "The other draw the pictures."
  Tom and Michel's book is about dinosaurs.
  "I'll be the author!" says Tom. "I'll start with T Rex!"
  "I'll draw!" says Michel.

Michel picks up a felt pen. He starts to draw the dinosaur.

"Not there!" says Tom. "Put him nearer the front." Tom points to the place where he wants the dinosaur to go.

"OK," says Michel. He starts again.

"Make his legs bigger," says Tom, looking across. "T Rex has long legs."

"OK," sighs Michel. He makes the legs bigger and longer with his green felt pen.

Tom gets on with the story.

"Now along comes Triceratops," he says out loud. "T Rex and Triceratops meet."

Michel carefully puts Triceratops into the background of the picture.

"No!" says Tom. "Not like that. They're meant to be having a fight."

Tom grabs a brown felt pen and tries to draw another Triceratops in the front of the picture.

"Get off!" snaps Michel, stopping him. "I'm doing the pictures! It's not just what you want!"

"They have to fight! It's in the story now!" says Tom.

Michel covers the picture with his hands.
Tom holds on to the story page. Both boys stop working.

"Ten more minutes left!" says Mrs Casey to the class.
"Then we can look at all the work you've been doing."

"We won't finish like this," says Tom.
"We'll have nothing to show," agrees Michel.
Both boys are quiet for a moment.

"I want a picture of the dinosaurs fighting," says Tom.

"I like this picture just as it is," says Michel. "Why don't we have the battle on the next page?"

"Yes!" says Tom.

Tom begins a new page of the story.
Michel draws a fierce dinosaur battle.

At the end of the lesson, everyone shows their work. Tom and Michel are first to hold up their book.

"Did you enjoy working in a pair?" asks Mrs Casey.

"It was hard at first – but we worked it out!" Michel tells her.

When there's a problem

When you are doing something you enjoy, it is sometimes easy to be bossy. You have a clear idea of what you want to happen. You want things done your way. But that could be a problem if others have their own ideas.

If there's a problem, stop what you are doing.
Let everyone say what they want. Talk about everyone's
ideas. Work out how you can all get some of what you want.

GALWAY COUNTY LIBRARIES

Problem Solving

The children in Mrs Casey's class solved their problems.
They remembered a few problem-solving ideas:

 Let everyone say how they feel

 Share information about what happened
and let everyone say what they want

 Be clear about what the problem is

 Talk about different ideas for sorting out the problem

 Agree on an idea together – and try it out!

This plan might help you next time you have a problem to
solve. Sometimes a problem may seem too big to tackle alone.
You might need to talk about it with an adult first.